AUDIO ACCESS INCLUDED
Recorded Piano Accompaniments Online

PLAYBACK+
Speed • Pitch • Balance • Loop

SINGER'S JAZZ ANTHOLOGY | HIGH VOICE

cole porter

Arranged by Brent Edstrom

Cover photo © Getty Images / Hulton Deutsch / Contributor

To access audio visit:
www.halleonard.com/mylibrary
Enter Code
2360-7137-4237-8187

ISBN 978-1-5400-4198-2

HAL•LEONARD®

Visit Hal Leonard Online at
www.halleonard.com

Contact us:
Hal Leonard
7777 West Bluemound Road
Milwaukee, WI 53213
Email: info@halleonard.com

In Europe, contact:
Hal Leonard Europe Limited
42 Wigmore Street
Marylebone, London, W1U 2RN
Email: info@halleonardeurope.com

In Australia, contact:
Hal Leonard Australia Pty. Ltd.
4 Lentara Court
Cheltenham, Victoria, 3192 Australia
Email: info@halleonard.com.au

ARRANGER'S NOTE

The vocalist's part in the *Singer's Jazz Anthology* matches the original sheet music but is *not* intended to be sung verbatim. Instead, melodic embellishments and alterations of rhythm and phrasing should be incorporated to both personalize a performance and conform to the accompaniments. In some cases, the form has been expanded to include "tags" and other endings not found in the original sheet music. In these instances, the term *ad lib.* indicates new melodic material appended to the original form.

Although the concept of personalizing rhythms and embellishing melodies might seem awkward to singers who specialize in classical music, there is a long tradition of melodic variation within the context of performance dating back to the Baroque. Not only do jazz singers personalize a given melody to fit the style of an accompaniment, they also develop a distinctive sound that helps *further* personalize their performances. Undoubtedly, the best strategy for learning how to stylize a jazz melody is to listen to recordings from the vocal jazz canon, including artists such as Nat King Cole, Ella Fitzgerald, Billie Holiday, Frank Sinatra, Sarah Vaughan, Nancy Wilson, and others.

The accompaniments in the *Singer's Jazz Anthology* can also be embellished by personalizing rhythms or dynamics, and chord labels are provided for pianists who are comfortable playing their own chord voicings. In some cases, optional, written-out improvisations are provided. These can be performed "as is," embellished, or skipped, depending on the performers' preference.

The included audio features piano recordings that can be used as a rehearsal aid or to accompany a performance. Tempi were selected to fit the character of each accompaniment, and the optional piano solos were omitted to provide a more seamless singing experience for vocalists who utilize them as backing tracks.

I hope you find many hours of enjoyment exploring the *Singer's Jazz Anthology* series!

Brent Edstrom

BEGIN THE BEGUINE

from JUBILEE

Words and Music by
COLE PORTER

ALL OF YOU
from SILK STOCKINGS

Words and Music by
COLE PORTER

ANYTHING GOES

from ANYTHING GOES

Words and Music by
COLE PORTER

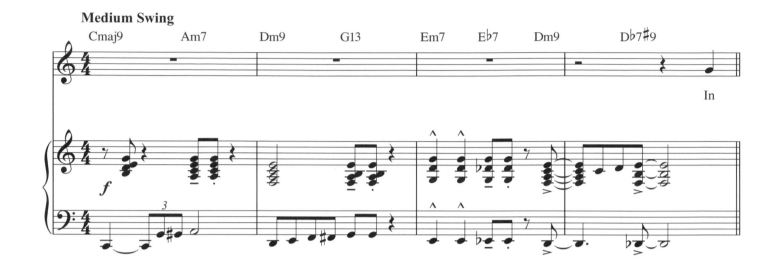

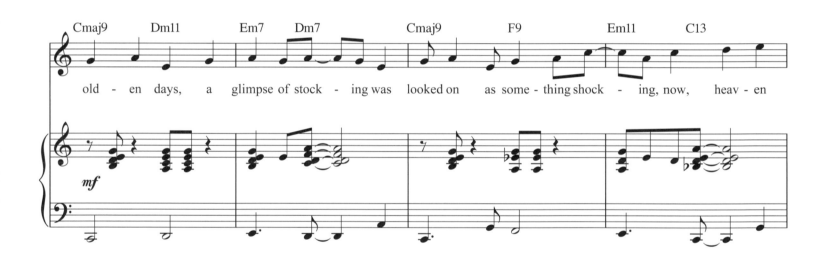

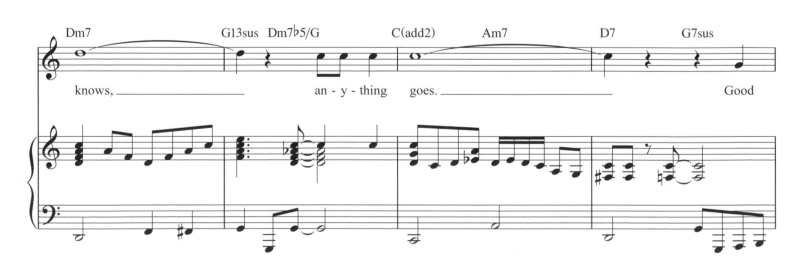

AT LONG LAST LOVE

from YOU NEVER KNOW

Words and Music by
COLE PORTER

EASY TO LOVE
(You'd Be So Easy to Love)
from BORN TO DANCE

Words and Music by
COLE PORTER

23

GET OUT OF TOWN

from LEAVE IT TO ME

Words and Music by
COLE PORTER

no - where you come to me as be - fore To take my heart and

break my heart once more.

Bright Swing

Get out of town ___ Be - fore ___ it's too late, my love; ___

___ Get out of town, ___ Be good ___ to me, please. ___

EV'RY TIME WE SAY GOODBYE

from SEVEN LIVELY ARTS

Words and Music by
COLE PORTER

FROM THIS MOMENT ON

from OUT OF THIS WORLD

Words and Music by
COLE PORTER

I CONCENTRATE ON YOU

from BROADWAY MELODY OF 1940

Words and Music by
COLE PORTER

When-ev-er skies look grey to me _____

and trou-ble be - gins to brew, _____

I'VE GOT YOU UNDER MY SKIN

from BORN TO DANCE

Words and Music by
COLE PORTER

48

I GET A KICK OUT OF YOU

from ANYTHING GOES

Words and Music by
COLE PORTER

I LOVE PARIS

from CAN-CAN

Words and Music by
COLE PORTER

Freely flowing

Ev - 'ry time I look down on this time - less town, wheth - er blue or gray be her skies, wheth - er loud be her cheers, or wheth - er

IN THE STILL OF THE NIGHT

from ROSALIE

Words and Music by
COLE PORTER

Gentle Rumba

In the still of the night, As I gaze from my win - dow, At the

IT'S ALL RIGHT WITH ME

from CAN-CAN

Words and Music by
COLE PORTER

IT'S DE-LOVELY

from RED, HOT AND BLUE!

Words and Music by
COLE PORTER

You can love - ly."

JUST ONE OF THOSE THINGS

from HIGH SOCIETY

Words and Music by
COLE PORTER

LET'S DO IT
(Let's Fall in Love)
from PARIS

Words and Music by
COLE PORTER

LOVE FOR SALE
from THE NEW YORKERS

Words and Music by
COLE PORTER

Freely

When the on-ly sound in the emp-ty street is the heav-y tread of the

heav-y feet that be-long to a lone-some cop, I _____

_____ o-pen shop. When the moon so long has been

88

NIGHT AND DAY

from GAY DIVORCE

Words and Music by
COLE PORTER

RIDIN' HIGH
from RED, HOT AND BLUE!

Words and Music by
COLE PORTER

Love had socked me, sim-ply knocked me for _____ a loop.

Luck has dished me Till you fished me from _____ the soup.

Now to- geth- er We can weath- er an- y- thing.

95

96

TOO DARN HOT

from KISS ME, KATE

Words and Music by
COLE PORTER

100

WHAT IS THIS THING CALLED LOVE?

from WAKE UP AND DREAM

Words and Music by
COLE PORTER

YOU'D BE SO NICE TO COME HOME TO

from SOMETHING TO SHOUT ABOUT

Words and Music by
COLE PORTER

YOU'RE THE TOP

from ANYTHING GOES

Words and Music by
COLE PORTER

Moderate Swing

At words po-et-ic I'm so pa-thet-ic that I al-ways have found ___ it best, ___ In-stead of get-ting 'em off ___ my chest, ___ to let 'em rest un-ex-pressed. ___ I

YOU DO SOMETHING TO ME

from CAN-CAN

Words and Music by
COLE PORTER